ISBN 978-0-259-43188-6
PIBN 10232069

This book is a reproduction of an important historical work. Forgotten Books uses
state-of-the-art technology to digitally reconstruct the work, preserving the original format
whilst repairing imperfections present in the aged copy. In rare cases, an imperfection in
the original, such as a blemish or missing page, may be replicated in our edition. We do,
however, repair the vast majority of imperfections successfully; any imperfections that
remain are intentionally left to preserve the state of such historical works.

1 MONTH OF
FREE
READING

at

www.ForgottenBooks.com

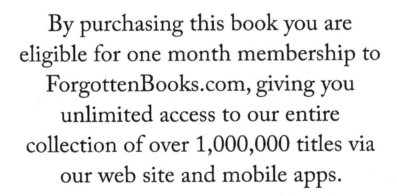

By purchasing this book you are eligible for one month membership to ForgottenBooks.com, giving you unlimited access to our entire collection of over 1,000,000 titles via our web site and mobile apps.

To claim your free month visit:

www.forgottenbooks.com/free232069

MEMOIR

OF

JOHN LEWIS RUSSELL,

BY

Burkee

EDMUND B. WILLSON.

[From the Essex Institute Historical Collections, Vol. XII, No. 3.]

SALEM:
PRINTED AT THE SALEM PRESS,
1874.

18 Oct., 1898.

FROM ESSEX INSTITUTE HISTORICAL COLLECTIONS, VOL. XII, NO. 3.

MEMOIR OF JOHN LEWIS RUSSELL,

BY

EDMUND B. WILLSON.

[COMMUNICATED MAY 13, 1874.]

JOHN LEWIS RUSSELL, son of John and Eunice (Hunt) Russell, and grandson of William and Mary (Richardson) Russell, was born in Salem, Massachusetts, Dec. 2, 1808, and died in the same town, June 7, 1873.

William, the grandfather, born in Boston, May 24, 1748, was a schoolmaster and adjutant of a regiment of artillery in his native town. He was a zealous patriot in the revolutionary period, was one of the "sons of liberty," assisted in the destruction of the British Tea in Boston harbor on the 16th of December, 1773, and later, having entered the naval service of the country, was captured and confined three years and more in Mill Prison, England.

John Lewis, the subject of this notice, was sent to the Latin School in Salem, in 1819. His father removing to

Amesbury the following year, he was for a time placed
under the tuition of "Master Pike" in the Academy at
Newburyport, but finished his preparation for college
under the instruction of the Rev. Mr. Barnaby of Amesbury, a Baptist clergyman. He entered Harvard College
in 1824, graduated in 1828, engaged in the study of the-
ology the same year, and graduated from the Divinity
School in Cambridge in 1831.

From 1831 to 1854, Mr. Russell occupied various Uni-
tarian pulpits for longer or shorter periods; among them
those in Fishkill, N. Y., Burlington, Vt., Pittsburgh,
Penn., Kennebunk, Me., Chelmsford, and the Second
(South) Parish in Hingham, Mass. In the last named
place he was settled for more than seven years continu-
ously, from June 26, 1842, to Sept. 1, 1849, and preached
there by extended engagements at other times, nearly
three years in all. In 1853, upon the death of his father,
he returned to Salem where he continued to reside till his
death, preaching only occasionally.

On the 4th of Oct., 1853, he married Hannah Buck-
minster Ripley of Greenfield, Mass., who survives him.
They had no children.

Mr. Russell's chosen profession, it will be seen, was
that of the ministry. Though he did not spend the greater
part of his active years in permanent pastoral relations
with any religious society, his heart was in this calling.
He was interested in theological inquiry and marked its
progress with a keen attention. He had great respect for
good learning, and never failed to pay due honor to true
scholarship. He held up before himself and others high
standards of training and attainment in the ministry;
and though his personal tastes led him persuasively to
the study of nature, and his deep moral convictions and
humane feelings impelled him strongly to certain forms of

philanthropic discourse and action, he set none the less
value upon patient research, sound criticism, and the fruits
of thorough professional culture. As a preacher his reputation was the best with the most thoughtful and advancing
minds, and his pulpit efforts showed vigor and ability.
We find him setting off for a distant state to preach in
the early part of his ministry, with the cheering assur-
ance of his teacher, the honored and beloved Prof. Henry
Ware, Jr., that he had no need to fear that he would not
find himself welcome and useful, provided he went "with
a courageous spirit;" that discerning counsellor adding:
"I am a little fearful that you want that *boldness* which
is necessary to the best action of a man's powers, and that
from your self-distrust you fail to put forth your utmost
strength." Concurrent with this judgment, is that of another early friend and distinguished scholar and preacher *
who writes since his death: "My impressions of him were
that he was a man of more ability than the world knew of,
of a singularly observing and acute mind, and of warmer
sympathies than he was wont to express. . . . If his personal ambition had been greater he would have attracted
more notice from the world."

At an early age Mr. Russell showed a marked fondness
for botanical observation and study. This interest was
materially strengthened during his college course by acquaintance with a few in Cambridge of similar taste. He
kept it, and it increased when he went out into the world
to preach. This pursuit was with him something more
than a recreation. Side by side with his ministerial work
it held its place in his regard without, however, causing
his earnestness in the minister's work to flag. It was some
five and thirty years ago that I first saw him. A lad

---

* Rev. Geo. Ripley.

sixteen or eighteen years old I was introduced into a clergyman's "study" in a country village in the north of Middlesex county. Somewhat familiar with the aspect of country clergymen's studies, I had never seen anything like this before. Of books there were enough; about the usual number of shelves and volumes, I think: I find I do not remember much about them. What I noticed more was that all the available room was filled with plants and flowers; green things and beautiful. In a corner stood fishing rod and tackle; and disposed in odd nooks, boxes, baskets, and cases, such convenient furnishing, it may be presumed, as the botanist and student of nature requires for his pursuits. The apartment was lovely as a garden; and when, presently, the minister who wrote sermons there, and there opened the books of God's Scripture and Revelation in many kinds, came in, he was one to whom the place seemed befitting; hearty in his greeting, fresh, natural, radiant with health, bubbling as a fountain with spirits and humor, as if he knew the woods and pastures and streams for many a mile round about, as no doubt he did. He stood like a brother among the stalks and plumes, Nature's own child,

Wherever this man went to fill a pulpit the lovers of nature gravitated towards him, and he made them his allies. They attended him to the fields, and ranged with him the steep hills and the miry swamps. His animated talk and moist kindling eyes as he described the graces of the ferns and the glories of the grasses and the lichens quickened the love of beauty in them. He imparted stimulating knowledge of the secrets of the meadows and woods, and drew about him by instinctive sympathy such as had an ear for the mysteries of the sea, or the forests, or the moss-coated rocks.

At the formation of the Essex County Natural History

Society in 1833, Mr. Russell was chosen Librarian and
Cabinet Keeper; in 1836 he delivered the annual address
before it; and in 1845 was elected its President, which
office he held till by its union with the Essex Historical
Society in 1848, the Essex Institute was formed, when
Judge Daniel A. White, the senior of the two presidents
of the societies merged in this, became the president of
the new organization, and Mr. Russell its vice president; in which office he continued till 1861. During the
greater part of this time, though not residing in Salem,
Mr. Russell gave much important aid to this society, under
its different names and organizations; and on his return
to make this city his home in 1853, he came at once into
direct and active connection with its work. At the "field
meetings" held at short intervals in various parts of the
county in the warm season, he was one of the most constant attendants and diligent explorers; and none contrib-
uted more largely than he to make them instructive and
entertaining. For several years he was also a frequent
lecturer and speaker upon his favorite theme before Nor-
mal Schools and other schools and institutions, and he
was never more radiantly happy than when surrounded
by young and eager minds thirsting for the knowledge he
could impart. Attentive faces roused him to glowing
enthusiasm and rapid speech; and many a listener dates
the birth of a life-long interest in natural history or in
scientific inquiry to his fascinating portrayal of nature's
wonders—of the order and beauty and endless transfor-
mations and creations of her realm. He held a high
place in the regard of men most instructed in the field of
his chosen studies. The best botanists of the country
ascribed to him, besides a general acquaintance with the
New England flora, an extensive and accurate knowledge
of the Cryptogamia in particular, and of lichens more

especially, in which department he ranked as an original worker and of the first class of amateur students. "He was an earnest naturalist," says Professor Edward Tuckerman, "who gave all his power to the explication of vegetable nature, and when he began, it was here in New England almost wholly neglected and unknown." "I always watched his career with interest," writes the accomplished scholar and joint-editor of the " New American Cyclopedia," George Ripley. . . . . "Of late years I knew him best by his contributions to the 'Cyclopedia.' They were of great value to the work, and an important element in the reputation which it has gained with scientific readers. In the revision in which we are now engaged I daily miss his aid and counsels."

In 1831 Mr. Russell became a member of the Massachusetts Horticultural Society ; and in September, 1833, was chosen Professor of Botany and Horticultural Physiology in that institution, succeeding Dr. Malthus A. Ward, who had held the office since the formation of the society in 1829. Professor Russell filled the office until his death, nearly forty years.*

' Mr. Russell maintained an extensive and interesting correspondence with naturalists at home and abroad, his opinion being often sought with deference by European botanists.

---

* Professor Russell delivered the Annual Address before the Society in 1835 ; prepared the Report of the Transactions for the years 1837-8, with Preliminary Observations ; Reports on Seeds from Prof. Fischer of the Botanic Garden at St. Petersburg ; and on Seeds from the Exploring Expedition in Transactions of the Society, 1842-3, p. 52, Dec. 2, 1842 ; Report on Seeds from Prof. Fischer, June 7, 1845 ; Transactions for 1842-46, p. 82 ; Report on the Distribution of Seeds by the United States Patent Office, Transactions for 1858, p. 97 ; an attempt at a Report of the committee on the Robin, etc., Transactions for 1866, p. 75 ; Report on Seeds from Northern India, presented by Rev. C. H. A. Dall, Transactions for 1868, p. 93.

Those only knew Mr. Russell well who knew him long, in the freedom of familiar and friendly intercourse, and when the circle was small. It was truly said of him that "his private friendships were dearer to him than public applause." He was transparent; not difficult to know by reason of any reserves, but rather liable to be partially known, and easy to be misunderstood from the variety and extremely wide range of his moods, in all which he needed to be seen to be comprehended. Thus one early teacher and friend who knew him intimately held him too self-distrustful, and needing boldness. Others knew him, or thought they knew him, as bold to the point of recklessness. He was both. And whichever he was at any moment, he showed it, for he could not disguise it. He hated shams and knew not how to conceal himself. In some hours he seemed the farthest going reformer, and most unsparing iconoclast, to whom nothing was too sacred for plain speaking, instant judgment, irreverent questioning. In other hours he was the tenderly religious, reverent soul, charitable in the construction of human motives, and living, as it seemed, joyously at home with the God of nature and all the great human family. Sometimes he was silent and shut in, his manner not inviting approach, and he passed along the streets with scarce a nod of recognition. At other times he was sunny, warm with kindness, and inclined to linger for conversation, in which he was racy, instructive, delightful. It is not meant that he was amiable and cordial to his friends, shut and cool towards certain he did not like; for he was inaccessible to the friend when the silent and unsocial mood beset him, and withheld himself from none when his central love glowed again and thawed all the rigors away. He was so scornful of pedantry and pretence that he would seem sometimes for the moment to

set light by real learning and culture of deservedly high
repute; and again he would honor with the heartiest
applause genuine scholarship; and always showed a pref-
erence, other things being equal, for men who had had
the training of the best schools, and especially for those
bred at his own, the Cambridge University, over the mis-
called "self-made" men, on many of whom his verdict
would likelier have been, not-made men. He was both
radical and conservative. What was peculiar was not
that he was sometimes the one and sometimes the other,
for most of us are by turns of a conservative and of a
revolutionary spirit, but that he went so far and so unre-
servedly each way for the time. He swung through such
a wide space in his oscillations, as startled men of a
colder and more cautious temperament, and puzzled their
judgment. The consistency and unity that was in him
was not outward, and did not lead to explanations and
the balancing of phrases. It was deeper; in his nature;
where he took in and assimilated the seemingly adverse
and contradictory. So he did not explain often when
expected to; did not see that there was need. He saw
at each moment his one thought, vividly, with his whole
concentrated attention, and uttered it. Why should he
stop to remember at the moment whether there were not
other things also that he thought true? Doubtless. But
he could not stop; the momentum was too great. He
was too full of *that*. And on he went, like the brimful
river, which cannot dally with its banks, but is driven
forward by force of its own weighty tide. It was not
strange that some knew him only as a radical of the radi-
cals; for sometimes he was that. He was that in the
utter freedom of his mind, and of his speculations.
Nevertheless he destroyed only that he might build the
better. He struck at what appeared to him error only

for the sake of truth. In terms he often misrepresented his own thought, to those who judged him by what he said at one hearing, and said extemporaneously. His thought was a feeling as well as a thought; a burning conviction; opposition only intensified its expression. Spontaneous, impetuous, unguarded, he neglected to state qualifications which were always a part of his mind, and which to one conversing with him privately and leisurely he would not fail to produce. This caused him often to be misunderstood. Tell him his own words, sometimes, and he would not recognize them. In his mind they had been joined with complementing truths which balanced and adjusted them, and which he felt that he must have stated or implied, but which he had only expressed on other occasions. He was called a "hard-hitter" in the field of theological controversy; and he was. Still he was no sectarian. The lovers of God and man, the people of sincere faith, those who made it the test of pure religion and undefiled before God to visit the fatherless and widows in their affliction, and to keep one's self unspotted from the world—these he took to his large heart with all the wealth of its trust and love. And there he cherished them, not caring by what name they were called. If they brought forward their sectarian passwords, or if in any manner these came in his way, he was very likely to visit on *them* his trenchant scorn; but he sincerely loved many people who used them and held them to be important. His spontaneousness and warmth gave expression to his prejudices equally strong and unguarded with the language in which his philanthropy found utterance, and equally laid him open to misconstruction at times. He was an earnest and uncompromising opponent of American slavery, at a time when slavery had many and powerful apologists in the northern states. He spoke out in hearty and ringing words against its wrong, and in

favor of freedom. The form of his plea was comprehen-
sive, taking in all humanity. But he had his dislikes.
There were traits in the Irish character which roiled him.
And sometimes, in his fashion of seizing a point and
pushing it to an extreme, he bore hardly on the people of
that race, not stopping to say that it was their faults
which he had presently in mind, and that there had been
untoward circumstances in their history that should be
had in mind in mitigation of a sweeping condemnation.
And this seemed an inconsistency by the side of his good
words for humanity, for all men without distinction of race
or color. But when others condemned the same people
too unsparingly, *he* adduced the mitigating circumstances.

It was truthfully said of him: "His was one of those
rare minds which loved truth and justice for its own
sake, and he was always ready to brave the loss of fame
or friends in behalf of what he deemed right. . . .
Did he but imagine any one was being trodden on who
deserved a better fate, he was ready to enter the lists in
his behalf at any cost. Often in these cases he could see
only the injustice at the moment; but after the struggle
was over, and he was alone or with intimates, the moist-
ure would rise to his eyes in the fear that in the contest
he might have hurt the feelings of those opposed to him."
The writer illustrates the last point by an incident. "An
article had recently appeared in high scientific quarters,
which was unfortunately inaccurate in its statements. In
his paralyzed condition he wrote, pointing out the errors,
but he added, 'in times past he has been at my house and
partaken of my hospitalities, and I would, under no circumstances, say anything to hurt his feelings; but in the
interest of truth and science you can do it at some time
without offence to any one.'"*

---

* The Gardener's Monthly for July, 1873: Philadelphia; p. 214.

I have written with freedom and unreserve of my friend. He was one of those whose character would bear it, while his own truthfulness and unreserve invited it. He preferred truth to compliment. There is no need to be timid and careful in speaking of one who was so much a man. To conceal or evade in speaking of him would be an offence against what was most characteristic in him, his sincerity and truthfulness of speech. His was one of those strong and capacious natures that hold the contents of two or three ordinary men, and combine such qualities as would be thought ordinarily to exclude each other. Men less intense than he, and of a more equable temperament, would have escaped strictures which he drew on himself at times; and so would they have failed to make the deep and lasting impression for good which he often made by his impetuous enthusiasm and almost passionate warmth of feeling and expression, in behalf of unrecognized truths. As his life wore on, however, and especially as the years of sickness fell upon him, the contrasted colors in his character blended and mellowed each other, and enhanced the sweetness and grace of his autumnal ripeness. He was always a lover of beauty—everywhere and of all kinds. Beautiful flowers, graceful ferns, such beauties as lay thick in his own chosen path—these of course, but not these alone. He felt the charm in all Nature's creations, animate and inanimate; the beauty of childhood; the beauty of young men and maidens; the holier beauty of truth, and moral strength and courage, the graciousness of goodness. He came at times as near reaching eloquence—that rare and subtile power impossible of definition—as almost any one I ever listened to. And the themes which kindled him most sympathetically and surely were those which lie about the fountains of worship, religious inspirations and moral integrity and order :—the universal care and tender

love of the divine providence, as witnessed in nature, in
life, in history:—human rights; the freedom of every
man to be himself, to think, judge, worship, unhindered.
That way of his, of putting his whole glowing soul into
the things he said; of forgetting himself; yielding himself
up to the grand inspirations of truth, righteousness, and
freedom — it was a deepening stream, gathering volume
and tide as it went, until it swept him and his hearers
along, seemingly, whithersoever it would.

His affections were deep and strong; and in his friendships he was close and fast. They had their full expression only when the sympathy was genuine and the
confidence without alloy. And the love and friendship
which he inspired grew to be like his own, tender and
true. It is not permitted me to invade the privacy and
sanctuary of his innermost communion with those he
loved, but it will be deemed no trespass upon that seclu-
sion, I trust, to make simple mention of the gentle affec-
tionateness that breathed from his lips, beamed from his
face, shone even through his veiled and half-blinded eyes,
and ran through his messages of friendship, and filled up
the hours, as his earthly life faded into that unseen realm
which seemed as real and present, as familiar, natural and
home-like to his thought, as the plans and expectations
of to-morrow. When asked what reply should be made
to a letter just received from a dear friend, he said :—
"Write, Love and Friendship; then turn over and write
on the next page, Love and Friendship; then on the next
write, Love and Friendship;" like John in his old age,
who, when too feeble to walk to the Christians' place of
assembly, asked to be carried thither only to repeat each
time, "My children, love one another."

During his last illness he was overfull of this sensi-
bility. Reminiscences of past friendships revived with
fresh tenderness and force. His playfulness was thought-

ful, his thoughtfulness playful, after the manner of his robust years; and through all there ran a vein of personal caressing and fondness when he spoke to his friends, or dictated words to be sent to them, which told how he held them to his heart.

To two old and dear friends he wrote soon after the new year :—

"Wasn't it a curious coincidence that I should have been busily engaged in trying to puzzle out some of the Dutch lingo of Van Sterbeeck's 'Theatrum Fungorum,' the gift of you, dear ———, at the time when your mutual gift of fruit and New Year's gratulations was in the expressman's care on its way to me? I wonder if there is such a book as a Dutch dictionary (Holland and English, or Dutch and French), for I am bound to read Sterbeeck, and to get all the good I can out of him. But, poor fellow, his effigy, on p. 35, looks as sober as I do most of my time; but, *sub Dio*—or Divine Providence, as you will—I am pretty well for a recluse, shut up in the house all the time. Your timely and very generous gift made me *cry* just a little bit, reminding me of you both, and of all the delicious memories of the olden time, when I used to know you so well, and many others who are in the great mysterious unknown, and who come to me in my dreams, and revive the days of youthful friendship in the old colony and elsewhere. What a strange, incomprehensible thing is this life, and what is it all for? God grant that I may wait and trust, for that is all I can do. But what treasures of love and of wisdom too have come to me in my sick chamber, and in the weary days and nights! Two things would I ask of God, viz.: health and the power and desire to love. There is no gift of love so trifling as to be insignificant, nor a breath of health which is not a magnificent fact of Providence. . . . . . I have a few friends with whom I talk of the probabilities of mutual recognition in the Hereafter, and of a closer friendship than can exist here. I hope I shall always know and love you both.

With much effort to write you this scrawl, and wishing
you a happy new year,   I am" ———.

Among children he was a child; and towards those
whom he had known in childhood he delighted to main-
tain afterwards the easy freedom and familiarity of tone
suitable to an elder brother, or companion-father, even
after they had arrived at the years of manhood and
womanhood.   Such he rarely addressed by other than
their christian names.   Indeed, he loved to borrow this
Friendly style in his intercourse with all whom he took
into his confidence and intimacy.   He loved to continue
the use of the terms and forms of endearment, of pet
names, and words of pleasant associations, first adopted
in his joyous talk and companionship with children, and
which he never after outgrew or laid aside.

A week only before he died he dictated the following
characteristic letter to one who had long held a place
close to his heart.

"MY DEAR LITTLE M. :—Although I am on my bed,
my thoughts are a great way off with you.   How I wish
you could come and sit by the side of your dear old
'lunky Jack,'* and we would talk about the old times
when you used to ride on my shoulder, and when you
were so much comfort to me; and though we are so far
apart, yet thought can travel faster than railroad speed,
and I can imagine that I am sitting beside my little M.,
and holding her hand, and her poor old 'lunky' is walking
with her, looking after the little flowers and thinking of
the good times we used to have together, which, if they
never come back to us, we can remember with great
delight and pleasure.   And may my dear little M. become
the dear friend, the upright and noble woman, a delight
to all who know her, patient with the weak, instructing
the ignorant, helping the poor to bear their lot in life,

---

* His pet name when M. was a child.

the sick to be patient and cheerful, the unfortunate to be full of hope and courage, the weary and broken-hearted to trust in God's love, the poor little destitute children to gain friends.

I am sick and faint in body, but strong in heart, never for a moment suffering myself to doubt the wisdom of God as shown to us in his constant providence, which makes us brave in life's duties, and trusting and hopeful to the end. . . . .

Remembering with pleasure the many happy hours I have spent with you, may your life, dear M., be full of happy recollections and bright anticipations, till in serene faith you pass to a more glorious life, where everything shall be tending to the perfection of all that is glorious in your nature.   Your own   LUNKY JACK."

In the foregoing letter he seems to be flitting between the present with its recollections, and that past to which he transports himself with such a vivid realization of it, that it seems to displace for the moment the present, and to become itself the present to his consciousness. I shall place before the reader extracts from one more similar letter, written about three months earlier, but when he was in very feeble health.

"SALEM, Feb. 23, 1873.

MY DEAR ———

When this reaches you spring will have commenced, and March winds, even if not zephyrs, will have awakened some of the sleeping flowers of the western prairies, while we shall be still among the snow-drifts of tardy departing winter. As I have not learned to fly yet I shall not be able to ramble with you after the pasque flower, or anemone, nor find the *Erythronium albidum*, nor the tiny spring beauty, nor detect the minute green mosses which will so soon be rising out of the ground. But I can sit by the Stewart's Coal Burner in our sitting room and imagine the daily changes which will usher in a milder spell of weather, and remind C. of ploughing and sowing and such occupations. Or I can recall the days when you were one of us, and when we gathered Andromeda buds from the frozen bushes and traversed the ice-covered bay securely in the bright sunshine of the winter's day.

I often long, dear S., for a return of those Arcadian days; . . . . . Sickness is no pleasure; and ennui and fatigue must come with it; but it is a blessed minister and teacher! It tells us of the excellence of health, and of the value of the slightest instance of love and regard.

. . . . As I grow older—now threescore and nearly ten—every year as it comes in regular order interests me all the more in his [God's] works and ways. Every little flower I meet with, and that I never saw before, every little insect which is a novelty—or as the naturalist would say is a new species to me—the constantly occurring microscopical forms of organized matter, the strange and veritable laws of the atmosphere, the clouds passing over the disk of the sun, and bringing to us storms and aerial phenomena, the ever-increasing discoveries of science and of art, awaken my admiration, heighten my awe, and lead me to adoring trust. How different, too, appear what narrow-minded men call religion, and the essentials of religious life, as I find good in everybody, and as I learn to draw nearer to my fellow beings in harmony with what is best in them. . . . .

I will not trouble you to write to me, but I should like a spring flower which you gather; any one will be precious from you to your feeble and sick

Old uncle and friend, J. L. R."

Our friend has drawn the lines of his own portrait truer than we could do it, and we leave it, as his own trembling fingers touched it, unconsciously, and left it at the last, radiant with trust and love.

"Contemplate all this work of Time,

. . . .

Nor dream of human love and truth
As dying Nature's earth and lime;

But trust that those we call the dead
Are breathers of an ampler day
For ever nobler ends." . . .

CPSIA information can be obtained
at www.ICGtesting.com
Printed in the USA
BVHW091120271118
534110BV00023B/1216/P

9 780259 431886